Grade 1

Scott Foresman

Decodable
Readers 25-36
Unit 3

INSTRUCTIONAL MEDIA CENTER
MEDFORD SCHOOL DIST. 549C
MEDFORD, OREGON 97501

PEARSON

Scott Foresman

Editorial Offices: Glenview, Illinois • Parsippany, New Jersey
New York, New York
Sales Offices: Needham, Massachusetts • Duluth, Georgia • Glenview,
Illinois • Coppell, Texas • Sacramento, California • Mesa, Arizona

ISBN: 0-328-14502-5

Copyright © Pearson Education, Inc.

All Rights Reserved. Printed in the United States of America. This publication is protected by Copyright, and permission should be obtained from the publisher prior to any prohibited reproduction, storage in a retrieval system, or transmission in any form by any means, electronic, mechanical, photocopying, recording, or likewise. For information regarding permission(s), write to: Permissions Department, Scott Foresman, 1900 East Lake Avenue, Glenview, Illinois 60025.

9 10 V054 14 13 12 11 10 09 08

Contents

Will They Get Here?

Written by Dylan Sacks
Illustrated by Peter Toomey

Phonics Skills

Long i: y		Long e: y	
my	Sy	buddy	Bobby
by	Dy	happy	
try	cry		

My name is Sy.
My buddy Bobby and
I will take a trip.

My mom and I got to
the plane by five.
Bobby and his mom, Dy, are late.

Bobby and Dy just met us.
"What made you late?"
I asked.

Bobby and Dy try
to wave at the bus.
The bus can't see them.

Bobby did not cry.
Bobby and Dy run
fast and catch up.

Bobby and Dy get off
when it stops.
They run and find us.

All of us get on the plane.
Bobby and I are happy.

The Picnic

Written by Chantell Brown
Illustrated by Olivia Hughes

Phonics Skill

Long Vowel Pattern: CV

no	go	be	Mo	he
Jo	hi	my	she	we

"No! I will not go!"
I said. "It will
not be fun."

"Mo will come," Mom said.
"Mo likes the picnic.
He will bring Jo."

"Will Jo and Mo
go now?" I asked.
"I want to see them."

I saw Jo and Mo.
I waved at them.
They yelled, "Hi!"

I asked my mom,
"Can I race with
Jo and Mo?"

She said,
"Yes, but be safe."
Mo, Jo, and I ran a lot.

When the sun went
down, it was time to go.
We felt tired and happy.

The Family Picnic

Written by Nicolas Florino
Illustrated by Dan Vick

Phonics Skill

Consonant Blends -nk, -ng

bring   drinks   trunk   swing(s)   sing(s)   songs

What will we do?
We pack food in a basket.
We bring drinks.

We sit on the grass.
Dad makes food.
Yum!

Next we run races.
We go to the van, and
then we run back.

20

Jan is fast!
She wins the race.
We are happy.

We rest by the tree trunk.
It is not hot.
It is a nice place to sit.

Mom and Dad help us
while we swing.
We like the swings and the slide.

At the end of the day, Mom sings songs. We sing with her.
It is time to go home.

Inside and Outside

Written by Carole Shannon
Illustrated by Kit Dunlop

Phonics Skill
Compound Words

inside	backpack	outside	sunshine
sunblock	treetops	sunset	bedtime

Pete has lots to do inside.
He feeds his fish.

He fills his backpack.
He eats his lunch.
He takes a nap.

Pete can go outside.
Pete has lots to do
in the nice sunshine.

Pete likes to jump.
He can jump rope.
He jumps and jumps.

Pete likes to swim.
He must use sunblock.
He can swim for a while.

Pete likes to fly his kite.
His kite will go up and up.
His kite is in the treetops.

At sunset, Pete must go home.
It is bedtime.
Pete has had a big day!

We See Pets

Written by Julie Marsh
Illustrated by Mickey Norton

Phonics Skill

Adding -es

rushes	classes	buses	dishes
fishes	kisses	foxes	wishes

Ken rushes down the steps.
All classes are going on trips.
His class is going to see some pets.

Buses line up.
Kids get on them.
This is it!

Patty has dishes to feed a rabbit.
Nick sees frogs.
He jumps like one.

Meg makes a fish face at fishes.
Jake sees a snake.
He steps back fast.

Jen kisses a puppy.
Kate said, "It is not a fox.
Foxes are not pets."

Ken sees a kitten.
He wishes that he had a kitten.

We must go back.
We had fun with the pets.

The Family Trip

Written by Mary Palmert
Illustrated by JoAnne Derbbs

Phonics Skill

R-controlled or, ore

wore	port	score	fort	shore
or	for	short	corn	more

I wore my cap.
I got my backpack.
We can go!

We are at a port.
I see ships in the water.

Dad and I see a ball game.
The score is six to five.

We drive to a big fort.
It has a big flag.

It is hot.
We can swim at the shore.
I can run or jump in the waves.

We go for a short walk.
We stop to eat clams and corn.
Dad has more clams than Mom.

We had fun,
but it is time to go!

Mom Races

Written by Jill Stanton
Illustrated by John Kircheff

Phonics Skill

Inflected Endings -ed, -ing

running	jogging	getting	jogged	sipped
asked	helped	standing	stopping	winning

Mom is running in a race.
She keeps in shape by jogging.

Getting in shape takes work.
Mom jogged five times last week.
She sipped water as she jogged.

I asked to jog with Mom.
She said it helped to run with me.
She gave me tips as we ran.

The race comes quick.
Mom is running a lot.

Dad takes me to the race.
We see Mom standing in line.
It is time.

Mom runs and runs.
She is stopping for a drink.
Is she winning?

Mom didn't win,
but she did her best.

Day at the Farm

Written by Jason Dee
Illustrated by Chris Brook

Phonics Skill
R-controlled ar

| farm | barn | hard | harm | cart | yard |
| smart | bark | dark | star | car | part |

Cass is going to see Kate and Mike.
They live on a farm.

Cass sees kittens in the barn.
She pets them but not very hard.
That could harm them.

Mike takes corn from a cart.
Cass and Kate feed it to hens
and chicks in the yard.

Smart pups bark at sheep.
The pups make them go in the pen.

As it gets dark, Cass, Mike,
and Kate look up.
Every star shines.

Mom honks the car horn.
Cass runs and gets in the car.

Cass likes the farm.
The best part is
seeing Kate and Mike.

A Big Day for Mom

Written by Bill Jones
Illustrated by Sarah Swanson

Phonics Skill

R-controlled er, ir, ur

stir	burn	her	dirt
ferns	curb	bird	chirp

Can we make Mom smile?
We have many wishes for Mom.

We will make Mom a cake.
We will mix and stir.
We must not burn her cake!

Mom is not afraid
to dig in black dirt.
Mom plants new things.

We have ferns for Mom.
We put them in pots on the curb.
Soon they will grow.

Will Mom like this bird?
It is big and green.

This bird lives in a cage.
Will this bird chirp?

See Mom grin.
She has a big smile.

Sam Can Fly!

Written by Lynn Johnson
Illustrated by David Newman

Phonics Skill

Contractions 's, 've, 're

you're   they're   she's   we've

Sam Bird felt small and sad.
"I cannot fly," she said.
She started to cry.

Dad patted her wing.
"One day," he said.
"These wings will fly."

Dad woke Sam the next day.
"You're a big bird.
You can fly!"

Sam hopped in her nest.
She felt happy.
"I hope I can fly!"

Mom came with Sam and Dad.
"Hop off with those fine feet, Sam.
They're so strong," Mom called.

78

Sam hopped off the branch.
The wind lifted her up.
"She's flying!" Dad yelled.

"She's flying!" Mom said.
"We've seen Sam try hard."

The Big Race

Written by Mark Bliss
Illustrated by Dan Vick

Phonics Skill

Comparative Endings -er, -est

hottest   taller   tallest   fastest

It is the hottest day.
The friends will
run a race.

June, Slim, and Gus line up by size.
Slim is taller than Gus.
Gus is taller than June.

"I am the tallest," said Slim.
"But I am the fastest," said Gus.
"Wait for me," said June.

"Let me help you," said Gus.
Gus used his trunk.
He picks up June.

"Go fast, Gus!
We can win this race,"
June yells.

Gus runs up and
down big hills.
Gus and June run by Slim.

The race is done.
Can you tell
who is faster?

Where Is My Badge?

Written by Erik Perez
Illustrated by Sandra Martin

Phonics Skill

Consonant /j/ -dge

badge   Madge   ledge   edge

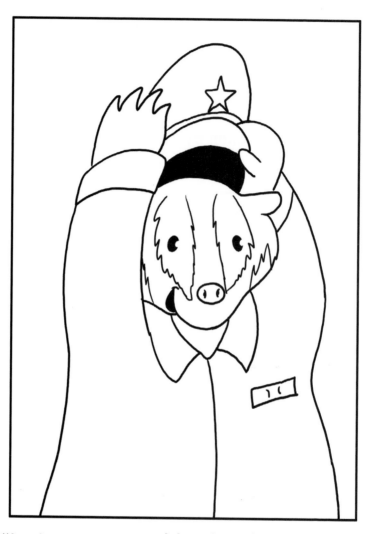

"Let's get my red badge first.
Then we can go,"
Bucky said to Madge.

"Where is my red badge?"
asked Bucky.
"I left it on that ledge."

"Is your badge on the edge
of that desk?" Madge asked.
"Did it fall in this trash can?"

"No," said Bucky.
He seemed sadder.
"We can't find my badge."

Madge sat on her bed.
Then she jumped up.
"I see it!" she yelled.

"It is by my brush," Madge said.
"Bucky, keep this badge safe.
It is your best badge."

"Thanks, Madge,"
Bucky said with a smile.
He felt glad.